MW00846749

ACCESSORIES FOR THE FOREDOM AND DREMEL FOR JEWELERS

Bradford M. Smith

Accessories for the Foredom and Dremel for Jewelers

All rights reserved. No part of this book may be reproduced in any form or by any means, electronically, mechanically, by photocopy, by scanning or otherwise without the written permission of the copyright owner. All illustrations, photographs, designs, and graphics are the property of the copyright owner.

The material in "Accessories for the Foredom® and Dremel®" should be used only as a learning guide. All generally accepted industry safety procedures should be followed when using tools in the jewelry shop. Nothing in these guidelines is intended to negate the need for proper clothing, masks, goggles, and other protection.

The Author and Publisher disclaim any liability for injury or unexpected results or problems that might occur while attempting to follow suggestions in this publication.

Copyright © 2017 - Bradford M. Smith

Published by Whimsey Wylde
Santa Monica, CA

ISBN-978-0-9882858-7-3

NOTE: Cool Tools, Dremel®, Foredom®, Gesswein, Lasco Diamond, OttoFrei, Prodigy, Proxon, and Wolf Tools are registered trademarks of their respective companies.

DEDICATION

For whatever artistic abilities I have in jewelry and photography,
I wish to give thanks to my Mom. For my underlying belief that
a person can accomplish anything they really want to do, I am
grateful to my Dad.

But the credit for continuing improvement of my skills in the
jewelry field must go to all my wonderful students over the years.
They are the ones who test my ability to clearly explain a topic.
They are the ones who improve my teaching with their insightful
questions. And they are the ones who offer me great feedback.
I learn as much from them as they do from me.

ALSO BY THE AUTHOR

BENCH TIPS FOR JEWELRY MAKING

BROOM CASTING FOR CREATIVE JEWELRY

MAKING YOUR OWN DESIGN STAMPS

THE RELUCTANT FARMER OF WHIMSEY HILL

http:// amazon.com/author/bradfordsmith

TABLE OF CONTENTS

PREFACE

1. OVERVIEW   1

2. DRILLING BITS   5

3. BURRING BITS   9

4. SANDING BITS   13

5. POLISHING BITS   23

6. TEXTURING BITS   31

7. MISCELLANEOUS BITS   37

8. DIAMOND BITS   41

9. MAINTENANCE & REPAIR   45

10. SAFETY   47

APPENDIX   INTERNET RESOURCES   49

ABOUT THE AUTHOR   51

OTHER BOOKS BY THE AUTHOR   52

PREFACE

The Foredom® flexshaft and the Dremel motor tools provide a tremendous help to those making jewelry, improving both productivity and quality of work. But selecting the best tool bits for a particular job can be a challenge for newbies. There are all sorts of tool bits in the catalogs with more being introduced by manufacturers each month.

As a jewelry teacher, one of my professional responsibilities is to stay current on the latest equipment in my field. So when I see or read about a new tool or process that might be of use for my students, I usually purchase one and test it out.

Based on lessons I've given on accessories for the flexshaft , this book identifies all of the tool bits typically used in the Foredom® or Dremel® motor tools at the jewelers bench. It will explain how each is used and offers my experience and recommendations for each.

The material presented here documents what I've learned from making my own jewelry, from teaching, and from feedback I've received from students. I'm happy to be able to put this knowledge into one volume for others who are interested in furthering their knowledge of jewelry techniques and metal arts methods.

Happy hammering!

- Brad

CHAPTER 1

OVERVIEW

Foredom® flexshaft and Dremel® motor tools are popular among hobbyists and professionals in a wide variety of fields. They are the mainstay of every serious model builder, wood carver, and of course, jeweler.

Both units, Foredom® and Dremel®, are relatively low power, have variable speed control, and make use of the same tool bits. The major difference, seen below, is that the Foredom® is usually hung next to the workbench and controlled by a variable speed foot pad.

This is a typical Foredom® installation, but the company has other units that vary in maximum speed and power to satisfy needs of different applications, and they offer a large number of different handpieces. See more about their different configurations and optional accessories at http://www.foredom.net/

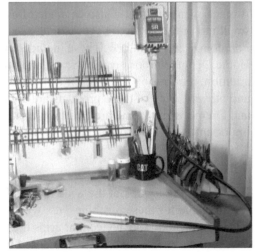

The basic configuration of the Dremel® is a hand operated tool with the speed control built into the body of the tool.

Dremel® motor tools are compact and very handy to pack in a toolbox for portable use. But the line also offers a range of accessories that allow it to be equipped with a flexible shaft and foot pedal speed controller to work at a fixed workbench.

If you travel a lot, you'll appreciate the battery operated Dremel® version that is a welcome addition to an on-the-road toolbox for classes, workshops, and shows. See more about their different configurations and optional accessories at https://www.dremel.com/

A quick mention should also be made of other manufacturers of small motor tools that are compatible with or similar to the Foredom® and Dremel®. These include units sold in the USA by Home Depot, Harbor Freight, Sears, and other companies. In addition, motor tools are offered worldwide by Proxon, Grobet, and others. Many of these products are compatible with Foredom® and Dremel®, but some are not. If compatibility of handpieces is important to you, be sure to check carefully.

Chucks

Before starting to look at the wide range of different tool bits that are available for these machines, it's worth understanding how the bits are attached. The device that grips the tool bit is called a chuck, and there are two basic types used by these motor tools - a collet chuck and a 3-jaw chuck. There are advantages and disadvantages to each.

Collet Chucks

The basic Dremel®, as sold, typically comes with a collet chuck that can clamp either a 3/32 or 1/8 inch size shaft. A wrench is supplied with the unit for changing tool bits.

Switching shaft sizes is done by inserting a different collet inside the chuck. Ordinary twist drills cannot be used in a collet chuck - only special ones like the drill shown above, which has a standard 3/32 or 1/8 inch shaft.

Adjustable Chucks

A 3-jaw chuck is adjustable and can grip a range of tool shank sizes. Shown above is one sold by Dremel® that grips a shaft up to 1/8 inch. It will also fit onto several other motor tools such as the

Craftsman unit in the center. Tightening the chuck is done easily by hand. No wrench or chuck key is required.

Adjustable chucks are inexpensive and enable fast changes between different size tool bits. They are available online or can be found in most large local hardware stores or model making outlets.

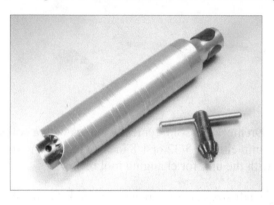

The Foredom® typically comes with a handpiece that has an adjustable 3-jaw chuck. It will grip a shaft up to 5/32 inch in diameter. The chuck requires a key to tighten the bit. Shown above is the H.30 handpiece. It also fits some other flexshaft tools such as those sold by Grobet and Harbor Freight.

Same Bits Used in Foredom® and Dremel® Chucks

The nice thing, from a jewelry perspective, is that both of these motor tools make use of the same tool bits that are sold by a wide range of companies worldwide. Low cost tool bits are key to the versatility of the Foredom® and Dremel® motor tools. But the problem for a newcomer is that there is a bewildering array of bits available.

In the ensuing pages I will itemize the bits typically used at a jewelers bench, explain how they are used, and will offer my experience plus recommendations for each. The explanations are organized along the lines of the five major operations where motor tools are most often used – drilling, burring, sanding, polishing, and texturing.

CHAPTER 2

DRILL BITS

Drilling is one the most common operations performed at the bench. Twist drills come in a multitude of sizes and are readily available even from local hardware stores.

The shank size on most drills is the same as the drill diameter. Therefore, an adjustable chuck is required on the motor tool. The popular Foredom® H.30 handpiece can accept drills up to 5/32 inches in diameter. The Dremel® adjustable chuck can accept drills up to 1/8 inch. And both can accommodate even the very small #70 drills.

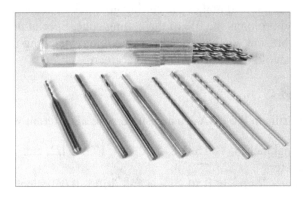

The only drills that can be used in a collet chuck or a quick-change handpiece are those with a standard size shank, 3/32 or 1/8 inch. A line of small drills (0.5 – 2.3mm) are sold in most jewelry supply catalogs that are made with 3/32 inch shafts to enable a fast tool change. These are high quality products with great cutting tips.

They bite in quickly wherever you position the tip which often avoids the need to center punch a divot to keep the drill from skating around before beginning to cut.

Buy Good Quality

Drills are made from a variety of steels which vary quite a bit in quality. When buying cutting tools, I avoid the cheapest as they are generally made from lesser quality steels. Those drills will dull rather quickly, lose their edge, and start overheating. The best drills in my opinion are high speed steel (HSS) for general work with copper, brass, silver, gold, and common steel. Cobalt drills are best for holes in harder steels or tougher metals like titanium.

I do not recommend carbide drills for general use at the jewelry bench. They are very sharp and seem like a good bargain. However, the steel is quite brittle, and the drills are easily broken off in a hole.

Use Lubricant

When using many cutting tools (drills, saws, and burs) to cut metal, it's best to use a lubricant. A little bit of oil, grease, or wax on the tip of the drill makes the cutting go quicker, keeps the tool cooler, and prolongs the life of the cutting edge. Special products are available, but you can use almost anything, including motor oil, olive oil, an old candle, or oil of wintergreen.

Drill Sizes

Sizes of drills in the USA are measured several different ways;

In fractional inches – 1/16, 1/8, 5/32, 1/4, 17/64, 1/2, etc.
In millimeters
By number – Range is 1-80 – i.e. a #53 drill is 0.0595 inches
By letter – Range is A-Z. – i.e. an "F" is 0.257 inches

Common sizes are given on "drill size charts" that can be found with a Google search. One example is at
http://www.gearhob.com/eng/design/drill_eng.htm

If drill sizes are important to your work, it's useful to have an accurate way to measure their diameter. A machinist micrometer or a digital Vernier caliper is worth the investment. And it also works for measuring sheet thickness, gemstone size, or prong and tube settings.

Broken Drills

If you ever break a drill off in a hole, you can sometimes grab it with pliers. But if the broken piece is below the surface in the hole, a quick fix is to dissolve the steel in a solution of new pickle or alum. This will not affect a piece made from silver or gold.

Alum is typically available from a food store. It's used to make a pickling solution. Use about a tablespoon per cup of warm water. Submerge the piece so that the partially drilled hole is facing up to let the bubbles float free and not block fresh solution from getting into the hole. Sometimes the piece of drill will dissolve enough in a couple hours to fall out, and other times it will take overnight.

CHAPTER 3

BURRING BITS

Often you need to cut away some material, be that plastic, wood, or metal. That's the job of a bit called a bur. It is a cutting tool made from HSS steel (High Speed Steel) with sharp teeth. Burs come in a variety of shapes and a range of sizes starting from a small 0.1mm (0.03 inch) like used by a stone setter or a dentist, up to perhaps 12mm (3/8 of an inch).

Burs are classified by shape and by size. The shape determines its major use. Within each shape, you can choose a range of sizes to match the pieces you work on. Finally, some burs come with fine teeth for precision work on metals, and others have coarse teeth for use on soft materials like wax or plastic that tend to clog a tool bit.

Burs are generally available only from large hobby or jewelry suppliers, so this means ordering from a catalog or from a website. My preferences, given in the Resources Appendix, are FDJ Tools, Otto Frei, and Rio Grande. Burs are generally sold in packs of six identical bits or as a boxed set with one of each size. As far as buying burs locally, some hardware stores will have a couple sizes sold under the Dremel® name.

Most Helpful Burs

The most useful shapes will of course vary with the work you do, but I would like to share the ones I've found that improve my productivity and let me get better quality at my bench. The burs I most frequently reach for include ball burs, cylinder burs, and inverted cone burs. These are all versatile and easily controllable.

Control is important to me. Some burs tend to grab and skitter across the workpiece. I hate it when this happens as it means a lot of extra cleanup time. Here are my favorites:

Ball Burs

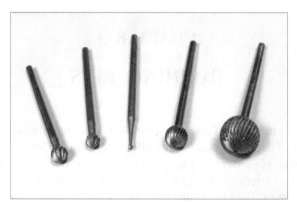

A ball bur is great for removing a lump of solder from a flat surface. The cutting area is limited to just the contact point between a sphere and a plane, so the area needing cleanup is small. They are also useful for beginning to cut a cavity or removing some excess material before using a setting bur. I use quite a range of ball bur sizes, the smallest being a couple tenths of a millimeter. It works nicely for marking a hole to be drilled or for signing your name.

The ball burs shown above are made of HSS but can also be purchased coated with diamond grit. These are usually used for lapidary work as mentioned in Chapter 8. But diamond being very hard can also be used to cut metal as in applying a surface texture as mentioned in Chapter 6. A diamond ball bur can also be used to smooth out the rougher tool marks left by an HSS ball bur when used to form a spherical cavity that will remain visible on the jewelry and thus needs to be polished.

Cylinder Burs

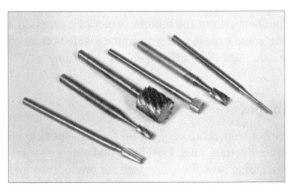

Cylinder burs are useful for operations like enlarging drilled holes, removing stock from the outside edge of a piece, and for shaping the outer edge of a cavity. Larger cylinder burs, greater than 8mm, are sometimes used as rotary files. All cylinder burs have teeth around the side. Some also have teeth on the bottom. Some do not. As far as sizes are concerned, I find there is little need to have a large range. A couple small ones (1-2mm dia) and a larger one (6-12 mm dia) seem to handle most everything I encounter.

Inverted Cone Burs

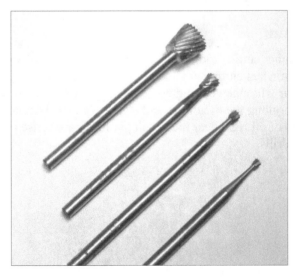

The last bur shape I find very useful is called an inverted cone bur. It has cutting teeth on the side and on the bottom. Most often they are used for cleaning out the bottom corner of a recessed area, such as removing some excess solder from the inside bottom of a bezel. But I have also used them effectively when carving a "V" shaped slot.

Other Shapes

Some other bur shapes are very useful for very specific purposes. One example is setting burs, Hart burs, and cup burs used in stone setting. Describing how these are used for prong, tube and flush setting requires a more lengthy tutorial than can be included here.

Other burs like rotary files, flame burs, wheel burs, bud burs, bearing cutting burs, and knife edge burs to name a few do exist but have very limited use in the type of work done in my classes. Any of the large jewelry supplies catalogs or websites will show the complete range that is available.

Caution is advised with the knife edge burs. They are hard to control and have a habit of biting in and walking around to the back side of a piece where your finger may be in the way. They cut quickly, and they cut deep.

Lubricant

As with other cutting tools such as drills and saws, it is best to use a lubricant when cutting any metal. Some oil, grease, or wax on the cutting bur will make cutting go quicker, will keep the bit cooler, and will prolong the life of the tool. Many jewelers keep a small bottle cap of oil right near the bench pin for frequent use on their burs and drills.

CHAPTER 4

SANDING BITS

I still remember how excited I was to discover the benefits of sanding disks and sanding drums used with the Foredom® or Dremel®. I consider them a tremendous time saver that lets me turn out much higher quality work. There are five general types of sanding bits that will save time with your work. Three are flat discs, and two are cylindrical drums. The flat disc types either have a center mandrel coming through the disc or are supported from the back. The cylindrical types are split mandrels or sanding drums.

Paper Discs

The basic sandpaper disc is mounted on a screw-on mandrel, the same type that is used to hold many polishing discs. Changing discs requires a small screwdriver to loosen or tighten the screw.

Sanding discs are inexpensive and come in a wide range of grit levels. Very fine grits can be found on those sold for working with platinum or those where the grit is bonded to mylar plastic discs.

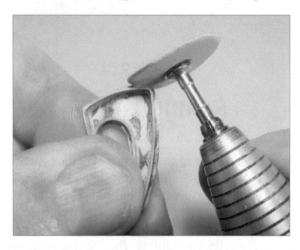

Ordinarily, you'd think of placing a sanding disc on the mandrel with the grit side facing away from your hand, but this often puts your elbow in an uncomfortable position. Instead, try flipping the disc so that the grit side is towards your hand. I've found this to be a very comfortable position with good visibility of where I'm sanding. My elbow is down by my side, allowing me to hold the workpiece up close to see what is going on.

Snap-On Discs

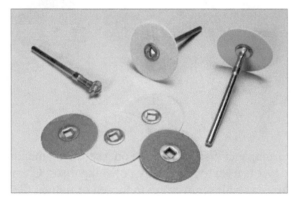

Snap-on discs make use of a springy bayonet mandrel that allows discs to be changed without the use of a screwdriver. One disc can be easily pulled off and another snapped on within seconds. Discs are available in a variety of grit sizes from coarse for rapid material removal, to fine and extra fine for smoothly finishing the piece before polishing. The backing sheet is typically a thick paper, a thin cardboard, or a tough plastic.

I keep four of these discs mounted on mandrels ready to go. Two are coarse grit, and two are fine. One of each is mounted towards the handpiece, and one of each is faced away.

If you have difficulty pushing these discs onto the mandrel or removing them, try squeezing the slot at the top of the mandrel. If that does not work, I use a fine file to remove the sharp points from the square corners of the mandrel. Only a very small amount has to be removed.

Stick-On Discs

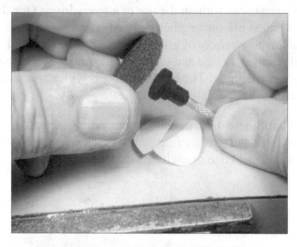

Stick-on discs come with an adhesive backing that holds the disc onto a special, flat-faced rubber mandrel. The main advantage of this type is that the whole sanding surface can be used. There is no screw head or snap-on mounting device to get in the way of using the entire surface of the disc.

EZ Lock™ Discs

The Dremel® EZ Lock™ system offers a larger flat sanding disc devoid of any center screw head. Discs are a generous 1.50 inches in diameter and come in 60 grit, 120 grit, and 240 grit.

The special Dremel® EZ mandrel allows discs to be changed out quickly without any tools required .

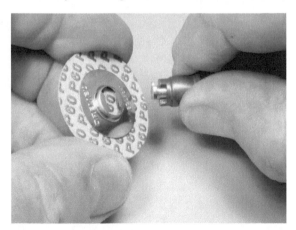

Changing a disc is most easily done with the mandrel fastened in the chuck. To attach or detach a disc, pull the mandrel collar back towards the chuck, insert the disc onto the mandrel, twist the disc 90 degrees either way, and release the collar.

Sanding Mandrels

These mandrels are split to allow strips of sandpaper to be inserted. That lets you use up assorted scraps and gives you a wide range of papers to choose from. This split mandrel is about 1/4 inch in diameter with a 3/32 inch shaft.

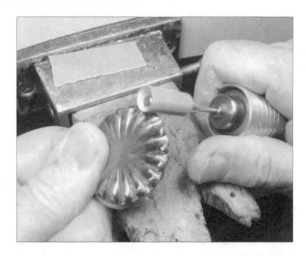

They are great for quickly rounding a sawed hole, finishing the inside of rings, or shaping the outside edge of thick material. I also find the sanding mandrels a good way to shape the bottom of a bezel wall for soldering it onto the curved surface of a bracelet.

Split mandrels come in larger diameters for bigger sanding jobs. This is the Kate Wolf sanding mandrel set sold by Wolf Tools, Cool Tools, EGGM Enterprises, Gesswein and others. Mandrel sizes start at about 1/4" and go up to 3/8" and 1/2" diameters.

Sanding Drums

The last popular type of sanding bit is the drum. Sanding drums are a good choice for removing or shaping soft materials like wood, plastic, and epoxy. They work well for finishing the inside of bracelets and rings, or removing excess sheet from around the bottom of a bezel cup. Sizes range from 1/4 inch to 3/4 inch diameter.

Sanding sleeves can be purchased in various grits. They are fastened by tightening a screw or nut on the end of the mandrel. A screwdriver or small wrench will be needed. This expands the rubber insert to grip the sandpaper sleeve securely. Larger sanding drums are available up to 3 or 4 inches but require a larger mandrel for use with an electric hand drill or bench mounted drill press.

Dremel® offers a unique mandrel that avoids the need for a wrench or screwdriver to change their 1/2 inch sanding sleeves. It is a push-pull device. Pull the sleeve away from the motor and the sleeve comes right off. Put on a new sleeve and push back towards the motor to secure it.

Other Considerations

A full range of grit levels is available with any of the above sanding bits. They may not be carried by the normal jewelry supply companies but can be found at suppliers to the lapidary trade or in a wider search on the Net. Some sources are included in the Resources Appendix.

The plastic discs are particularly nice and are available with abrasive grit that extends down into very fine grits if needed. Because they are waterproof, these discs may be used with a water spray for finishing lapidary and gemstone materials.

CHAPTER 5

POLISHING BITS

In the finishing sequence, there's a step called pre-polishing which is between sanding and buffing. One of the most effective tools I've found to help here is the little 1-inch diameter silicone rubber wheels. Available in several different abrasive levels and shapes, these wheels are color coded to denote their abrasive level. Different shapes (coin, knife, cylinder, point, etc.) are available to match the geometry of the area being cleaned up.

For a starter, I'd suggest a medium, a fine, and an extra fine wheel in both the coin shape and the knife-edge shape. Most jewelry catalogs carry the wheels, but understand that the color codes are not the same across different manufacturers. I use a line called AdvantEdge from Rio Grande where Medium is black, Fine is blue, and Very Fine is pink.

Choose the shape that matches the surface you want to polish. I find the thicker coin shapes are particularly handy for smoothing a curved surface such as a bezel. Cylinder shapes are nice for doing the inside of rings. Knife-edge shapes clean up the outside base of bezels quickly. And the small pointy shapes are great for getting into tight places. Be careful when using the more aggressive grits to keep the tool moving around so as to not dig any little ruts.

The knife-edge and the pointed bits are great time savers but tend to wear down quickly. The natural thought is to grab one of your files and hold it up against the rotating wheel to reshape it. Be careful because the grinding grit in the silicone wheel is much harder than steel, resulting in grinding down the teeth of your file.

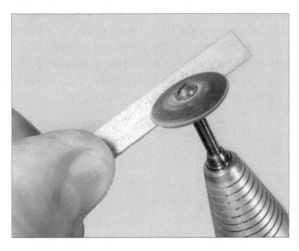

The best way to reshape polishing wheels is to use a diamond file. If you don't have one, sacrifice the area of your steel file that is closest to the handle. This is rarely used in normal bench work.

Polishing in Tight Places

On some pieces, you may occasionally find a few small areas in need of polish that cannot be reached with a 1-inch wheel. A pin polisher is a 2 or 3mm plastic rod that is held in the motor tool by a special mandrel. The rod comes in several color coded grit levels.

The pin polisher is made for getting into tight places where other polishing bits will not reach. I don't have to use it often. When I do, there are few alternatives to avoid a lot of work hand polishing with rouge or Zam on a chopstick or toothpick.

Cloth Wheels

Some jewelry is so delicate that it is risky to try polishing it on the regular polishing lathe. In these situations, small one or two inch diameter cloth wheels are available to use on the motor tool. This lets you use the same polish compounds but more carefully. If there's a chance you won't remember which compound has been used on each buff, just mark it on the cloth.

Felt Wheels

Felt buffs can be used for final polishing or just adding highlights. Some polishing compounds work better with a little pressure, and the harder felt does that nicely. Felt is less likely than a cloth buff to go down into recesses. This will preserve any patina that has been applied to the work. A light buffing with a hard felt wheel will just polish the surface highlights.

I have used hard felt wheels very effectively with diamond grit and/or diamond paste to carefully fix a scratch on a stone without having to remove it from the bezel. I start with a coarse 220 or 330 grit. Spread the paste onto a felt wheel or mix the loose grit with some oil or Vaseline and spread that onto the wheel. Similarly, I make up finer wheels with 600, 1200, 8000, and 14,000 grit for the polishing sequence on the stone.

If you try this technique for polishing gemstone carvings, take care to avoid any contamination of a coarser grit into the next finer grit wheel. After finishing with a coarser grit, I store the grit, the wheel, and the mandrel in a separate plastic bottle or baggie. I then thoroughly wash the gemstone and tools I used, and finally I wash my hands. Only then do I proceed with the next finer grit.

Brush Bits

Brushes can be used for cleaning and polishing. They come in two basic forms - wheel types with the bristles fanning out radially and cup or pencil types with the bristles along the axis of rotation. Some are made using wire bristles and some are made using plastic or natural fiber.

I use metallic brushes mostly for cleaning. Steel brushes are more aggressive than ones made with brass wires. The cup or pencil types do a nice job of cleaning out pockets or reaching into cramped spaces, while the wheel types make easy work of large areas.

Fiber brushes are generally used with a polishing compound like Tripoli, Zam, or rouge. They will get into crevices and hard to reach areas where a buff will generally not be as effective.

Bristle Discs

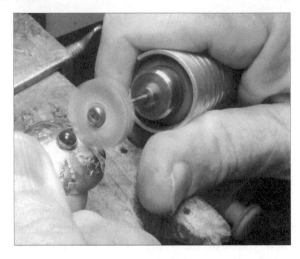

The bristle discs from 3-M are a novel polishing tool. Abrasive grit is mixed into the plastic that forms the bristles. They come in a good assortment of grit levels. Again color codes indicate the grit level of each brush.

Red   220 grit

Blue   400 grit

Pink   1,200 grit

Peach   3,000 grit

Mint Green   14,000 grit

The blue (400 grit) does a nice job at pre-polishing, the pink (1200 grit) begins the polishing, and the peach (6 micron) and the light green (1 micron) finishes it well. You'll like the way these discs reduce the amount of dust and lint from buffing. A side benefit is that you don't have to wash off any waxy grime between grit levels.

Bristle discs work very well if used properly. The most common errors are not mounting 3-6 identical brushes on each mandrel or putting the brushes on backwards so that the bristles get mashed as soon as the disc is used the first time.

The discs come in larger sizes as well - 2-inch or 3-inch diameters and in thicknesses of 3-ply or 6-ply. This makes them ready for use on a buffer or a yard sale motor that's fitted with a tapered spindle adaptor.

Buffing is one of the dirtier operations in making jewelry. If you have an electric buffer and work inside the home, buffer mess from lint and polish can be a problem. Of course you can buy a dust collecting system, which are large, noisy, and expensive. The larger bristle discs are a much more affordable solution.

I use the larger sizes at the jewelry bench I have at home. And since there is not much extra space, I mount them on my Foredom® using a 1/4 inch bolt and nut as a mandrel in an H.44T handpiece.

On a final note, safety glasses and a dust mask are prudent choices when using any of these polishing tools. The debris that comes off is a cloud of minute airborne particles that can easily get in your eye or down into your lungs.

CHAPTER 6

TEXTURING BITS

Adding a mechanical finish to one or more surfaces can often enhance the design of your work. First, it adds visual interest to sharpen the contrast between the polished and textured areas. Textures also serve a practical function, particularly to provide a non-slip grip or to hide fingerprints on a piece that is frequently handled.

There are many ways to add a texture to the surfaces of your work. Some techniques, like roll printing or stamping, apply a texture to the flat sheet at the start of the project. But a number of other techniques use bits in the motor tool to texture after the piece is nearly finished.

Brass and Steel Brushes

One of the easiest textures is a satin finish applied with a brass or steel brush. In applying textures, the coarser the wires in the brush, the more prominent the texture produced. Coarse steel wire types are the most aggressive. Brass brushes made from thin wires will give the most subtle satin finish. Brass brushes should be kept wet with soapy water to avoid any of the brassy color being transferred to the surface of the jewelry.

Diamond Ball Bur

Another type of satin finish can be applied with a 4mm diamond ball bur. Simply stroke the ball bur across the metal surface in a linear direction with a light constant pressure. Repeat with overlapping linear strokes until the whole surface is covered.

Sanding Disc

A "slashed" pattern can be applied with a sanding disc by first polishing the surface and then repetitively touching just the edge of the disc to the piece at varied angles.

Texturing Tool

These texturing tools are a little expensive, but are worthwhile if you do a lot of texturing of your sheet material before making jewelry and do not have the equipment to roll print.

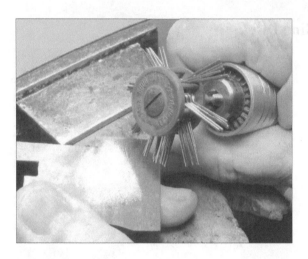

Caution is advised with this tool. You do not want to put a texture on your fingers. I would suggest holding smaller pieces with pliers, wearing a full face shield, and not over-revving the flexshaft.

Hammer Handpiece

A hammer handpiece on a Foredom® converts the rotary motion from the motor into a woodpecker motion at the tip of the handpiece. This is used to drive an anvil point for operations like stone setting. With just a little practice, setting a difficult or a thick bezel becomes remarkably easy.

When using a hammer handpiece, it is important to not rev the motor too fast. This generates excessive heat and wear in the mechanism. Also be careful not to bend the flexshaft sheath or the spring on the handpiece too much.

Anvil points, like any new tool, will need a little touch-up when initially purchased. I break the sharp edge around the tip, give the top surface a fine sanding, and then polish the tip on the buffer with Zam or Tripoli. The result is a nice anvil point for setting bezels, shown as #1 on the far left.

Spare anvil points can be purchased and shaped for other operations such as texturing. Each hammer blow then creates a repeated element of a fine texture on the surface of the jewelry item. Textures will look best if the hammer blows are random and are the same density across the entire surface. Try to avoid straight lines of the texture element as they tend to catch the eye. I try to keep the anvil point moving in small circles.

Hammer texturing is very handy because it can be done at any stage of completion in the jewelry construction process, even after final polishing. Anvil Points #2 and #3 were shaped with medium and large rounded tips for producing two different hammered textures. Anvil Point #4 was given a sharp tip for producing a stippled texture.

Anvil Point #5 on the far right is a little different. It has a small diamond set upside down at its tip. The point is called a pave tip for producing a bright, reflective texture pattern. #5 is available from most large tools suppliers. The texture looks great on gold or silver. However, it eventually tarnishes on Sterling and cannot be repolished.

CHAPTER 7

MISCELLANEOUS BITS

Separating Discs

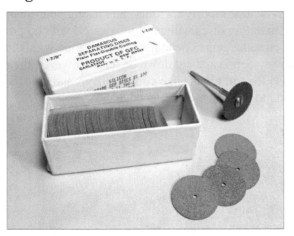

Often called a cutoff wheel, these thin abrasive discs are
inexpensive and do a great job at cutting, grinding or shaping steel.
You can use them like a miniature grinding stone to sharpen tool
points, cut steel wire to length, make slots, and sharpen worn drills.
My preference is the 7/8 or 1-inch diameter size. They are
available from any good jewelry tools supplier.

Other uses include modifying tools and making your own design stamps. Separating discs will cut through steel with no problem at all and even some gemstone materials when used with a little water to wash away debris and cut down on dust. However, the discs are not as good for soft metals like copper, silver, and gold. Soft metals tend to clog up the cutting edge.

Separating discs have only one problem. They break easily. When using these discs, be sure to hold the tool and the workpiece firmly so that neither moves to break the disc. And definitely wear your safety glasses. Those are little flakes of metal coming off the disc.

Grinding Bits

For anyone who has purchased a Dremel® kit, these coarse bits are a common sight. They are used primarily for grinding hard metals like steel, not the soft copper, silver, and gold that jewelers usually work with. Softer metals tend to clog up the cutting edges of the bits. However, these grinding bits do a nice job on hard metals like steel, so they can be very useful when making or fixing some of your own metal tools.

Like other abrasive bits, these grinding points come in different shapes and coarseness levels. Choose the shape for the desired cut and the grit level for the speed of metal removal and the final surface you desire.

Small Burs and Polishing Points

It may come as a surprise, but your dentist is using some of the same burring, sanding, and polishing bits as you are, except the ones used in your mouth are much smaller. They typically have a 1/16 inch shaft size (which fits into an adjustable chuck with no problems).

You may want to have a chat with your dentist to see if any of these tools might be of use in your work. My dentist gave me a couple sample bits above that he had decided not to use.

CHAPTER 8

DIAMOND COATED BITS

Diamond coated tools will cut or shape any other material.
Remember the hardness scale? Diamond is at the top, and industry
uses them for a host of jobs in manufacturing and construction.
Diamond abrasive grit is used for all gemstone processing and in
many forms at the jewelers bench. Diamond sandpaper, diamond
discs, diamond files, and diamond burs are commonplace and
readily available in a variety of grit sizes.

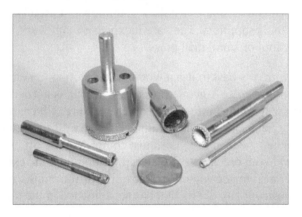

One of the most common diamond tools used in the Foredom® or
Dremel® is a core drill used to make a hole in hard materials like
glass, ceramics, and pebbles. We also drill cabochons for mounting
a stone onto a stone. This is done with water to wash away debris,
to keep the bit cool, and to minimize dust - which is not good to
breathe.

Core drills are more efficient than diamond coated twist drills because they are made from a hollow tube. However, accumulated cutout debris can be a pain to clean out of a core drill that has a blind hole. Frequent cleaning is essential, so I only buy core drills that have a through-hole for easy cleaning. The through-hole lets me push out debris quickly with a steel wire, an old drill, or a steel rod.

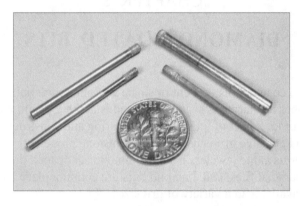

Core drills are available as small as 1.5mm from Lasco Diamond and other tools suppliers. They are inexpensive and work very well in a motor tool or small drill press.

When cutting, it's best to use a woodpecker motion to help clear debris from the hole. A gentle pressure is all that is needed. The diamonds will do the cutting. Too much pressure will cause a build-up of heat, causing the diamonds to come off the cutting surface. When the drill hole is almost complete, ease off on the pressure to avoid breaking off material from around the exit hole. Remember also to occasionally remove the drill from the motor tool and push out any debris that has accumulated in the through-hole.

I usually just use the bottom of a plastic bottle large enough to contain the workpiece. Leave enough of the sidewall on the bottom to be able to submerge the workpiece. It's a little messy, so use some plastic sheeting or a tray to contain the occasional spills.

Other shapes of diamond tools let you easily round the edge of a stone, cut a groove in a rock, sharpen a cutting blade, or reshape the end of a piece of hardened steel tool.

CHAPTER 9

MAINTENANCE & REPAIR

You may never have a problem with a Foredom® or Dremel® motor tool. They are solid, well proven designs that rarely cause any problems. Even if you do encounter one, company websites have good videos to help you fix it quickly.

I have several of both motor tools, and problems have been almost nonexistent over almost 20 years. On both tools, I do check the condition of the motor brushes about once a year. They are easily accessible with a small screwdriver. They will wear down with usage and should be replaced before they get too short. I order new brushes when I notice their length getting down to about 1/4 inch.

On the Foredom®, I look at the adjustment of the center shaft that drives the handpiece. It should poke out of the sheath by only 3/4 inch (19mm). Fine adjustment is done by loosening the screw up where the sheath joins the motor. Foredom® has some nice videos on its website that show all the details of how to do it.

My yearly check also includes lubrication of the flexible shaft. I clean off the old grease and add new coating from the tube they provide with all new units. Again, see the videos on the Foredom® website for the details.

CHAPTER 10

SAFETY

Rotary tools have several risks that can get you hurt. First, the rotational direction tends to throw debris directly at the user. Safety glasses and a dust mask are prudent choices for anyone who values their long-term health.

Secondly, using a cutting bur like a wheel bur or a knife-edged bur without thoroughly bracing your hands and the workpiece to control the cut often lets the bur grab and run off the workpiece where it can dig into a misplaced finger.

The third situation I see in class too often just leaves you shaking your head. When drilling a small hole, the drill breaks through and goes right into a finger holding the workpiece. Watch where your fingers are positioned or better yet, use a block of wood on the back side of the piece being drilled.

There is another safety risk that is not as obvious. When using a tool bit that requires applying side pressure, such as in grinding or polishing, it's best to purchase sturdy mandrels that will not bend. Many mandrels are made from nickel plated brass. They may look the same as steel but do not have the strength. In these applications use a steel mandrel and think about going to the larger 1/8 inch shank.

The reasoning behind this caution was an accident in class where a student was using one of the coin-shaped silicone polishing discs at high speed and was applying a fair amount of side force. The shaft bent and on its next rotation started battering fingers to the point we thought an X-ray might be needed.

APPENDIX

INTERNET RESOURCES

http://www.Foredom.net   The Foredom® Company

http://www.Dremel.com   The Dremel® Company

http://EGGMenterprises.com   EGGM Enterprises, Torrance

http://www.FDJtool.com   FDJ On Time, Winter Park, FL

http://www.LascoDiamond.com   Lasco Diamond, Calabassas

http://www.OttoFrei.com   Otto Frei Jewelry, San Francisco

http://www.RioGrande.com   Rio Grande, Albuquerque

ABOUT THE AUTHOR

Brad Smith is a studio jeweler, lapidary, and jewelry instructor in Santa Monica, CA. He enjoys working with silver, gold, exotic woods, bone, fossil ivory, and meteorite.

As a long-time member of the Culver City Rock Club, Brad has taught lapidary skills, led field trips to the desert, organized gem and mineral shows, and served in most of the club positions, including President. He is also a member of the Metal Arts Society of Southern California.

His teaching career started in the Los Angeles school system where he taught Advanced Jewelry in the Adult Education Department for eight years. Then in 2009, he was invited to design and build a new jewelry facility at the Santa Monica Adult Education Center where he currently teaches beginning and advanced classes.

Brad also likes photography & scuba diving, develops websites, and moderates several jewelry making and rockhounding discussion groups on the Internet.

Contact the author at
<AuthorBrad@yahoo.com>

or see his website at

http://BradSmithJewelry.com/

Thanks to My Readers

If you have enjoyed this book, could you please do me a favor and leave a few words of review on Amazon? Thank you.

OTHER BOOKS BY THE AUTHOR

Making Design Stamps for Jewelry

Learn how to create unique stamps and texturing tools to add visual interest to your work, for a special application, or to brand your pieces with a stamp that others cannot purchase. These customized tools embellish your jewelry designs and can be made with common jewelry tools and techniques. There are only a few differences in working with steel as compared to copper or silver.

The volume covers the step-by-step process of selecting best steels, carving the design, hardening the steel, and tempering it to ensure a long service life. It describes the tools to use, gives detailed examples for making several stamps, includes sources for tool steel, describes useful shop equipment, and has tips for saving time and achieving better quality.

amazon.com/dp/098828586X/

Editorial Review

"A must have book for the metalsmith"
   - Danny Wade, Ferro Valley Tool, LLC and
   creator of the Metal Stamp Addicts group on Facebook.

Amazon Reader Review

- This book is absolutely wonderful! If you are at all interested in the very least in making your own jewelry stamps, then you definitely need this book. At 68 pages, I was initially hesitant, but I was wrong; this book is jam-packed with a plethora of information, all of which is totally relevant, and revealing

Bench Tips for Jewelry Making

In every field, the top artisans have their favorite ways of solving common problems. Making a piece of fine jewelry is no exception. Accomplished jewelers have a variety of techniques, special tools and shortcuts that are proven to save time and improve quality.

This book is written as a resource for jewelers with skill levels from beginner through advanced. The bench tips come from Brad Smith's twenty years of experience in the jewelry industry, including over a decade teaching hundreds of students.

The tips include over twenty ways to save time when soldering and polishing, eight common hazards to avoid, many ways to cut costs, ten tips to improve stone setting skills, and the "must-have" tools for increasing productivity at the bench.

amazon.com/dp/0988285800/

Editorial Reviews

This small treasure covers a multitude of solutions to a myriad of issues facing the jewelry artisan…The easy to understand text and very good photographic black and white images makes this book quite self-explanatory…
> - Razine Wenneker - Founder, The Society for Midwest Metalsmiths

This is a well written reference book by a very experienced studio jeweler and classroom instructor. The photographs and diagrams clearly point out the finer points of the various tips he demonstrates…
> - Bruce Carlson - Florida Society of Goldsmiths Newsletter

Broom Casting For Creative Jewelry

Discover the rush of pouring molten silver into a straw broom to get marvelous icicle-like shapes that just beg to be designed into finished jewelry like pendants and earrings.

Broom casting is a technique that yields beautiful results, doesn't require a lot of time to learn, and is just plain fun to do. In a couple hours you can be producing intriguing geometries that spark the imagination and challenge your creativity.

"Broom Casting For Creative Jewelry" gives step-by-step procedures for casting and covers proper use of all equipment. It includes how to work with the irregular shapes for your designs and has suggestions for safety, tips for cleaning & polishing, and ideas for making some of your own tools. Other sections cover how to run your own broom casting workshop for friends & club members and a gallery of finished jewelry utilizing some of the cast shapes.

amazon.com/dp/0988285835/

Amazon Reader Reviews

- I've found Broom Casting a little intimidated, but I love the look. So I was really excited to hear about this book. Brad Smith's book really takes the mystery out of the process. He breaks down the steps really well, and walks you through the process clearly and simply. Then he shows you how to look at, clean/cut, and finally create with the castings. He really covers this cool technique from top to bottom. It's all in this great little book.

- Broom Casting for Creative Jewelry and Metal Work outlines everything you need to know to start and continue broom casting silver.

The Reluctant Farmer of Whimsey Hill - A Memoir

The Reluctant Farmer of Whimsey Hill is a light-hearted, true love story between more than a man and a woman. Imagine *Marley and Me*, not with one pesky dog, but with a farm full of quirky animals. The narrative follows Brad's fish-out-of-water point of view as a 25-year-old, animal-phobic, computer nerd from the city who moves to a rural, Virginia farm with his new, animal-loving bride. There he's propelled on a journey of self-discovery as his bride's crazy animals teach him about life and love - the hard way.

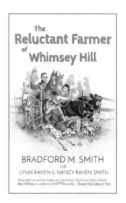

amazon.com/dp/0988285851/

Editorial Reviews

- Animals can and do make our lives better. This is my kind of book.
> - Bret Witter, #1 NYT bestseller co-author of Dewey [the Library Cat]

- A witty memoir reminding us that the best lessons in life are beyond the edge of one's comfort zone, and one can only be towed there by the heart strings."
> - Jean Abernethy, creator of Fergus the Horse

Amazon Reader Reviews

- Anyone who loves animals, has a sense of humor and appreciates a good, clean book (plenty of mud though) will love this book!

- A charming, witty, well written account of the country life of a young couple, with some sweet moments and some laugh out loud moments. We thoroughly enjoyed it.

Made in United States
Troutdale, OR
03/21/2024

18624767R00037